GUITAR SHEETS
TAB PAPER

The Missing Method
An imprint of
Tenterhook Books, LLC
Akron, Ohio

Christian J. Triola

Discover what you've been missing.

Copyright ©2024, 2020 Christian J. Triola, Amy Joy Triola

All Rights Reserved.

Except as permitted under the U.S. Copyright Act of 1976, no part of this publication may be reproduced, distributed, or transmitted, in whole or in part, in any form or by any means, or stored in any form of retrieval system, without prior written consent of the author.

Bulk sales inquiries can be directed to the author at info@themissingmethod.com.

Cover and Book Design by Amy Joy, ©2020 Amy Joy

The Missing Method™ for Guitar is an imprint of Tenterhook Books, LLC. The Missing Method name and logos are property of Tenterhook Books, LLC.

First Edition 2020, Tenterhook Books, LLC. Akron, Ohio.

Print ISBN-13: 978-1953101105 (Perfect Bound)

Table of Contents

Introduction 1

TAB Paper 3

TAB & Staff Paper 85

Appendix 117

    How to Tune Your Guitar 118

    How to Read Tablature 121

    The Elements of Reading Music 122

    Basic Chords 126

    Basic Scales 127

    Resources to Help You Take Your Playing Further 128

    Join our Growing Community 130

    About the Author 131

Introduction

Welcome to The Missing Method's blank tablature sheets for guitarists! In this book you'll find 80 pages of blank tabs for writing down songs, ideas, riffs, or anything else that comes to mind.

More than just tablature, this book also includes 30 additional pages of tab plus staff paper, as well as a reference section, which includes guitar basics like reading notes, understanding tablature, basic chords, basic scales, and other useful information!

Remember: besides practice, nothing helps you learn and process new information better than taking time to write things down! This book is more than just a place to record your ideas—it's a companion in your journey of musical discovery.

So, enjoy this creative space, and don't forget to visit TheMissingMethod.com for more tools to build your guitar knowledge and skills.

Happy playing!

Chrisitan J. Triola

TAB Paper

TAB PAPER

TAB PAPER

TAB PAPER

TAB PAPER

TAB PAPER

TAB PAPER

TAB PAPER

TAB & Staff Paper

92

94

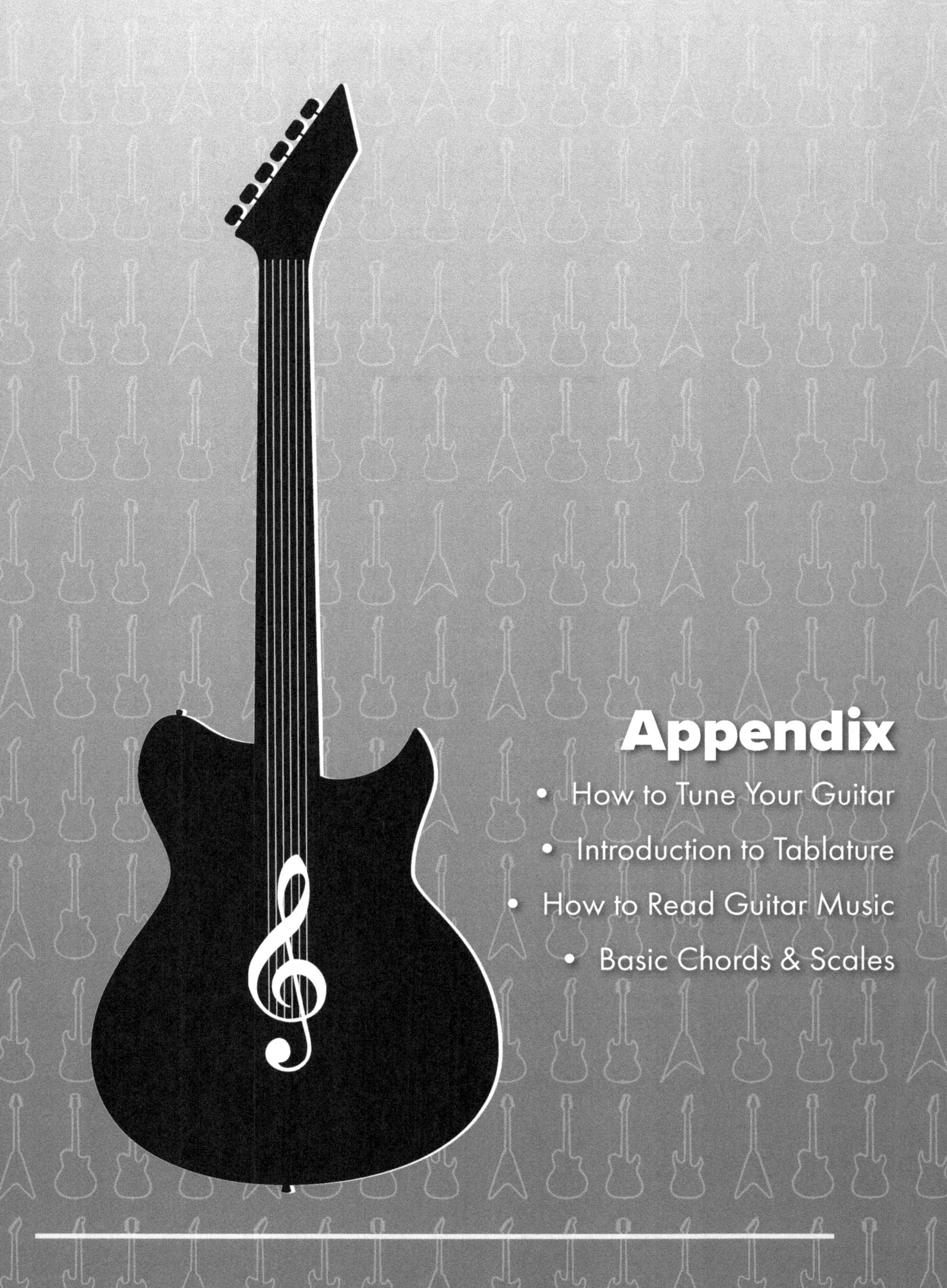

Appendix

- How to Tune Your Guitar
- Introduction to Tablature
- How to Read Guitar Music
- Basic Chords & Scales

How to Tune Your Guitar

1 The first thing you need to know in order to tune the guitar is what notes to tune to. The chart below shows the pitches of each string. Of course, if you are playing left-handed, these are reversed.

There are a couple of sayings that can help you remember the names of the strings, from thick to thin:

Eddie **A**te **D**ynamite, **G**ood **B**ye **E**ddie.

Or the less violent:

Every **A**mateur **D**oes **G**et **B**etter **E**ventually.

2 The second thing you should know is that tuning takes practice. It can be a little frustrating at first, but once you've done it a few times it gets easier and easier.

3 The third thing you need to know is that most of the time your guitar will only need slight adjustments. Once it's in tune, it will usually stay fairly close to in tune most of the time. However, it is recommended that you check your tuning every time you pick up the guitar. Be sure to listen carefully to the sound of an in-tune guitar so you become familiar with what it should sound like.

4 Now that you know this, we can begin tuning the guitar. There are several tuning methods. The best method is to buy a guitar tuner and learn how to use it. (You can find information on tuners on the next page.)

Typically, most tuners will show which note you are playing and then tell you whether or not the note is too low, too high, or in tune. Usually, a meter of some kind will display this information.

If the string is too low, you'll want to tighten the string, If the string is too high, you'll want to loosen it. Be sure to listen to the sound of the string as well. Your ear will help you figure out if you are going too far from the in-tune note.

Guitar Tuners and Other Tuning Resources

Tuners come in all shapes and sizes. There are credit card sized tuners, apps, and clip-on tuners that attach to your guitar. There are also good tuning apps available, and many of them are free.

Another way you can tune the guitar is to use a reference pitch from an instrument that is already in tune. Most people use a piano, another in-tune guitar, or a pitch pipe to achieve this. In this case, you simply listen to the reference pitch and then match that pitch on your instrument. This can be difficult for beginners, but can help you to develop a strong ear as well as help you to develop your overall musicianship.

If you struggle with tuning, please keep at it and remember that it gets easier with practice. If you check your tuning each time you sit down to play, you'll get better at it faster and enjoy the benefits of a well-tuned instrument.

For more information on tuning, be sure to check out The Missing Method YouTube channel. There you will find video tutorials on how to tune your guitar as well as how to keep your guitar in tune.

Find it at: YouTube.com/@TheMissingMethod

How to Read Tablature

Tablature (or TAB) is the most popular way of learning new songs. It is almost as old as standard notation for stringed instruments. The advantages of TAB are that it's easy to read and allows you to figure out songs much faster than standard notation. However, there are some drawbacks. Most TABS do not include any rhythm, meaning you have to either know how the song is supposed to sound ahead of time or rely on the standard notation, when available.

Tablature shows you *where* to play, while standard notation shows you *what* to play. Therefore, both are equally as valuable when learning a new song.

To read tablature, each line represents a string on the guitar. The lowest string is the bottom line, and the highest string is the top line. (See below). Numbers are placed on the lines to show you which fret or frets to place your fingers. For example, if you see a number 1 on the first string (the top line), simply play the first fret on the first string. A zero tells you to play the open string.

When reading tablature, the numbers on the lines represent the fret numbers.

The Elements of Reading Music

The Staff

Long ago there was no universal system to keep track of what a song sounded like. For a very long time, the only way to have a record of a song or piece of music was to pass it on from musician to musician by ear. Eventually, someone decided to place a circle on a line and call it a specific pitch. After some time, more lines were included, and the modern staff was born. The **staff** is simply a chart showing the highness and lowness of pitches. The lower a dot (or notehead) is on the staff, the lower the sound and vice versa.

In order to know which range of pitches to perform, clefs were used. A **clef** is a symbol that tells what notes to expect on the staff. There are several clefs in music, but for guitar we only need to learn one: the **treble clef**. (Though it is recommended to learn bass clef as well in order to develop your overall musicianship.)

Staff with Treble Clef

The treble clef tells you what specific notes, or pitches, you can expect to find on its lines and spaces. The lines are (from low to high) E G B D F. The spaces are F A C E. Many elementary schools teach a mnemonic device to help you remember these note names: Every Good Boy Does Fine. And of course the spaces spell FACE.

Ledger Lines

It is possible to go higher and lower than what is on the clef. When this is done, the extra notes are placed on lines called **ledger lines.**

In music there are a total of 12 notes that can occur at different pitch levels. Each different sound is given a letter name. Thus the musical alphabet consists of A B C D E F G. However, this represents only seven of these notes; the remaining five notes fall in between these and are designated either sharp or flat.

Understanding Time

The staff is divided up into sections called bars or measures. This is done to make the music easier to read and to help you figure out when to play the notes.

Each measure is only allowed a certain number of notes. This limitation allows us to keep track of time. The grouping of these notes is called meter. The most common meter is four beats per measure, or 4/4 time.

Beat is the underlying current of the music. You don't necessarily hear the beat. Think of it as a second hand on a clock, a constant steady clicking that helps you keep track of time.

What you actually play is **rhythm**. Rhythm tells you how long or how short a pitch should be held. For example, in 4/4 time a whole note is sustained for four beats. A half note is sustained for two beats. A quarter note (which takes up a quarter of a measure) is sustained for only one beat.

Besides 4/4 time, the second most common meter is 3/4. This means that there are only three beats per measure, instead of four, and the quarter note still represents the beat.

Eighth Notes

A quarter note can be further broken down into two eighth notes, each representing half a beat. When performing eighth notes, pick down on the downbeat, and up on the second half of each eighth note pair.

Eighth Notes

Sixteenth Notes

Eighth notes can be further broken down into four equal parts called sixteenth notes. That means that you can now play four notes for each beat. Just like eighth notes, sixteenth notes are often played using alternate picking. When counting sixteenth notes they are pronounced like this: One Eee And Uh, Two Eee and Uh, etc.

 If you'd like to learn more about note reading, check out The Missing Method for Guitar Note Reading Series. It'll take you through every note in every key!

Basic Chords

Basic Scales

Major Scale

Natural Minor Scale

Harmonic Minor Scale

Minor Pentatonic Scale

Major Pentatonic Scale

Resources to Help You Take Your Playing Further

Perfect Practice

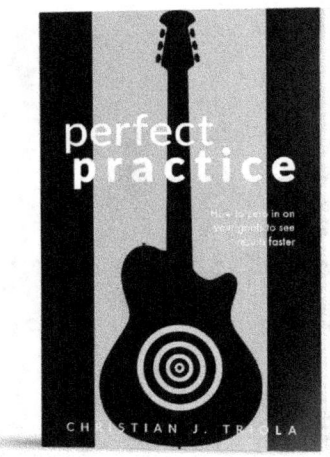

Rethink how you practice. Stop practice burn-out. Learn the secrets to transforming your practice time into time well-spent. This book will help you to figure out how to identify and overcome the obstacles in your way by showing you what to practice and how to structure your time so you see results faster.

Guitar Chord Master Series

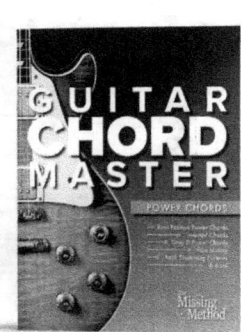

Guitar Chord Master is the only method book series that focuses exclusively on learning chords and strum patterns. Each book takes you step-by-step through the process of learning chords in a musical context, allowing you to master them for life! The series covers open chords, power chords, barre chords, how to use a capo, moveable shapes, and much more. Available in right and left-handed editions.

Technique Master Series

  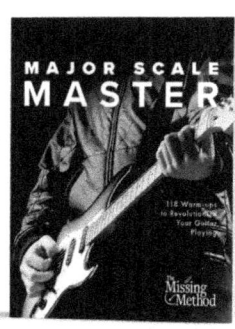

Avoid injury and learn how to play the right way with the Technique Master™ series. Build finger strength, dexterity, and knowledge of the fretboard with warm-up exercises, scales, licks, arpeggios, and more. Discover the difference a good set of warm-ups can make!

The Missing Method for Guitar Note Reading Series

    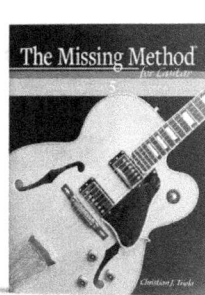

Designed with the serious guitar player in mind, The Missing Method for Guitar Note Reading series teaches you how to read every note on the guitar, from the open strings to the 22nd fret. If you are looking to master the fretboard, this is the series for you! Available in right and left-handed editions.

Discover what you've been missing

TheMissingMethod.com

Welcome to
The Missing Method for Guitar Community!

We're dedicated to helping you master your instrument. To that end, there are a couple of resources we want to make sure you are aware of:

The Missing Method for Guitar Monthly Newsletter

We only send out one a month, and you won't want to miss the updates on new and free resources, discount promotions, and more. Sign up at TheMissingMethod.com/newsletter.

The Missing Method for Guitar YouTube Channel

Here you'll find free weekly lessons on a variety of topics, including tutorials on how to play your favorite songs. Find it at: YouTube.com/@TheMissingMethod.

About the Author

Christian Triola is a guitar teacher and author committed to making guitar learning easy. Over his 20+ year career, he has taught thousands of people using a scaffolding approach that enables skill development through supportive instruction. He holds a Master's in Education and Bachelor's in Music (Jazz Guitar). When he's not teaching or playing guitar, Christian can be found writing fiction or hiking with his wife, Amy Joy.

What is the Missing Method?

We're more than just a guitar method. We're a family-owned company passionate about empowering aspiring musicians like you.

For over a decade, our step-by-step instructional materials have helped thousands of students, just like you, achieve their musical dreams. Whether you're a complete beginner strumming your first chords or a seasoned player looking to refine your skills, we offer a variety of resources designed to fit your needs and learning style.

Dive into the fundamentals with our self-guided books and courses for beginners. Learn essential skills like note reading, scales, and chords with our in-depth books and online classes for more experienced players. **Our structured, skill-building approach ensures you'll progress faster and develop true mastery.**

We believe in the power of music to change lives, and we're here to guide you every step of the way.

Discover what you've been missing at **TheMissingMethod.com**.